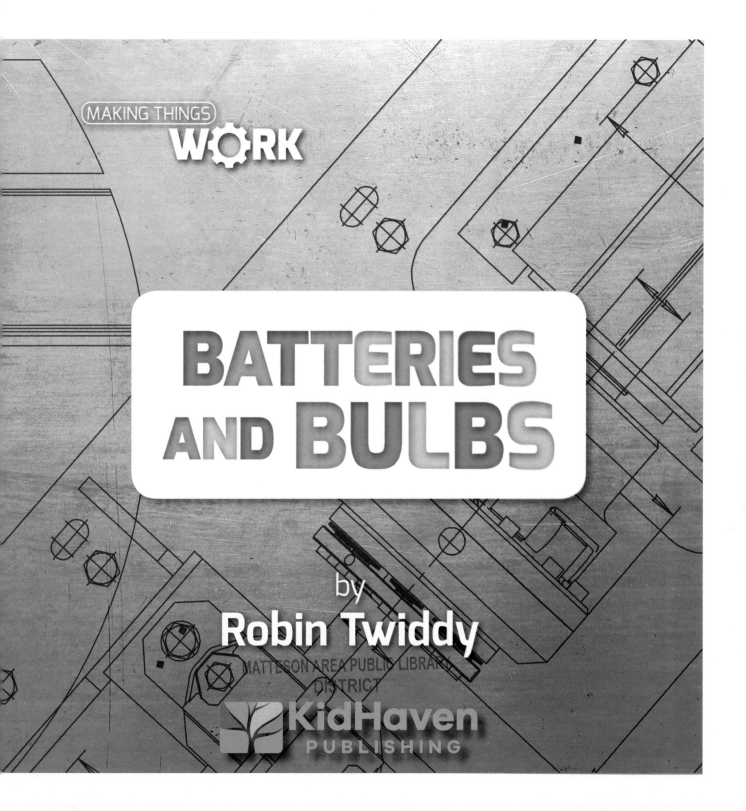

MAKING THINGS WORK

BATTERIES AND BULBS

by
Robin Twiddy

KidHaven
PUBLISHING

MATTESON AREA PUBLIC LIBRARY DISTRICT

Published in 2019 by KidHaven Publishing, an Imprint of Greenhaven Publishing, LLC
353 3rd Avenue, Suite 255, New York, NY 10010

© 2019 Booklife Publishing

This edition is published by arrangement with Booklife Publishing.

All rights reserved. No part of this book may be reproduced in any
form without permission in writing from the publisher, except by a reviewer.

Written by: Robin Twiddy
Edited by: Kristy Holmes
Designed by: Gareth Liddington

Cataloging-in-Publication Data

Names: Twiddy, Robin.
Title: Batteries and bulbs / Robin Twiddy.
Description: New York : KidHaven Publishing, 2019. | Series: Making things work | Includes glossary and index.
Identifiers: ISBN 9781534529359 (pbk.) | ISBN 9781534529373 (library bound) | ISBN 9781534529366 (6 pack) |
ISBN 9781534529380 (ebook)
Subjects: LCSH: Electric batteries--Juvenile literature. | Light bulbs--Juvenile literature. | Electricity--Juvenile literature.
Classification: LCC TK2901.T963 2019 | DDC 621.31'242--dc23

Printed in the United States of America

CPSIA compliance information: Batch #BW19KL: For further information contact Greenhaven Publishing LLC, New York, New York at 1-844-317-7404.

Photocredits: Abbreviations: l-left, r-right, b-bottom, t-top, c-centre, m-middle. All images are courtesy of Shutterstock.com.

Cover – tr3gin, Yuganov Konstantin, rakimm, PR Image Factory, Tatiana Popova, imagedb.com, pinkeyes, BalancePhoto, doomu, wb77, Dino Osmic, darezare, 2 - Chones,
4 – Smileus, 5 - wk1003mike, 6 - Chystopoltseva Kateryna, 7 - Nadya Kubik, Vereshchagin Dmitry, 8 - Kenishirotie, 9 - haryigit, 10 - art_photo_sib, 11 - Pra Chid, 12 - oxanaart,
Ivaschenko Roman, Serenethos, Tony Stock, Operation Shooting, 13 - Marcos Mesa Sam Wordley, 14 - Africa Studio, 15 - cooperr, 16 - imagedb.com, 17 - Photobank gallery,
18 - ZayacSK, 19 - SCOTTCHAN, 20 - mnowicki, 21 - MarchCattle, 22 - Parilov, antishock, 23 - Syda Productions, Radu Bercan, DeshaCAM, Icatnews.

Images are courtesy of Shutterstock.com. With thanks to Getty Images, Thinkstock Photo and iStockphoto.

All facts, statistics, web addresses and URLs in this book were verified as valid and accurate at time of writing.
No responsibility for any changes to external websites or references can be accepted by either the author or publisher.

CONTENTS

Words that look like this can be found in the glossary on page 24.

BATTERIES

A battery is a type of **container**. Batteries hold **energy** until it is needed. You probably have lots of things that use batteries in your home.

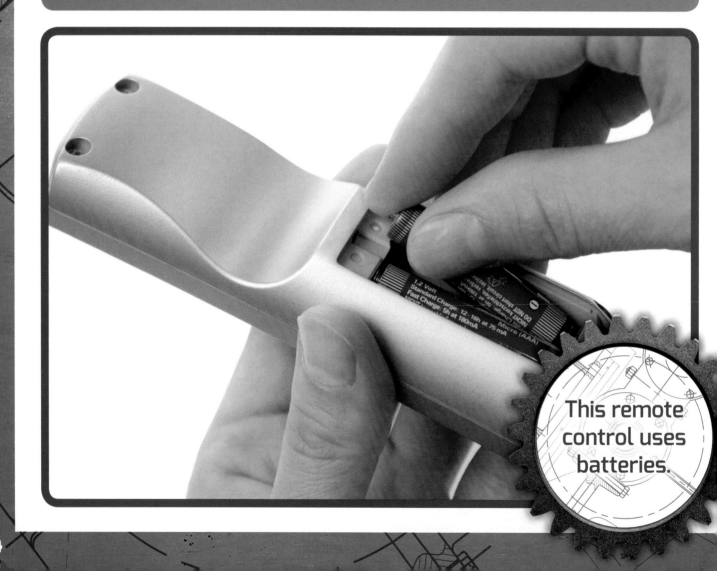

This remote control uses batteries.

Different Types
of Batteries

Batteries come in different shapes and sizes. Some are round
and some are rectangular.

WHY WE USE BATTERIES

This remote-controlled car uses batteries because they are **portable**.

We use batteries to give energy to things that use electricity to work, but can't be plugged in to the **grid power** supply.

Small things like watches use small batteries. Big things like cars use big batteries. Even very big things like airplanes use batteries.

Small Round Battery

Big Square Battery

HOW BATTERIES WORK

One end of the battery is called the positive end and has a small plus sign (+). The other end of the battery is called the negative end and has a minus sign (-).

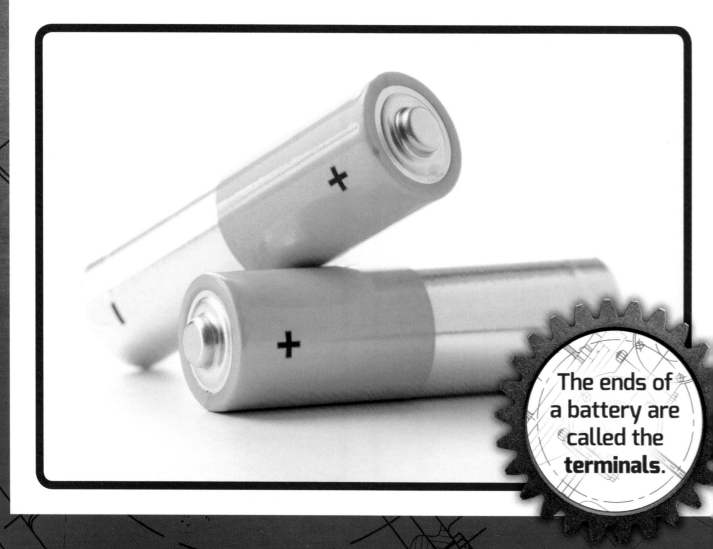

The ends of a battery are called the **terminals**.

The battery powers the bulb!

This battery is part of a **circuit**. The energy can flow from one end of the battery to the other, and around the circuit.

RECHARGEABLE BATTERIES

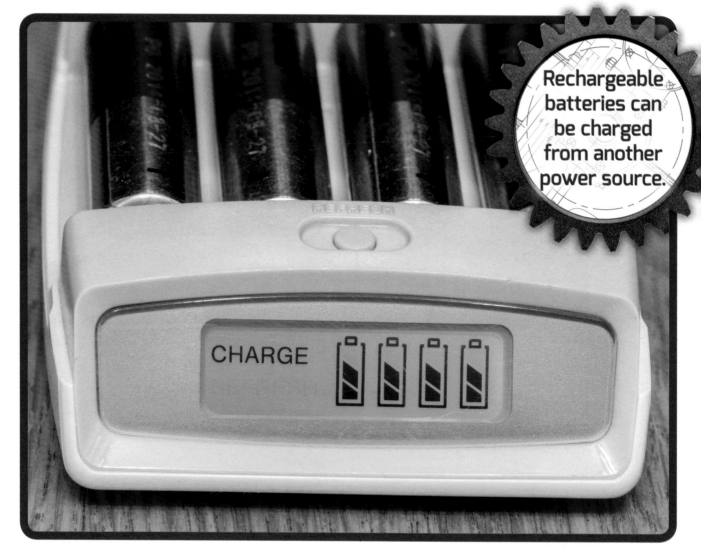

Rechargeable batteries can be charged from another power source.

CHARGE

Some batteries are rechargeable. This means that when they have run out of energy they can be filled up with more energy.

Some electrical items, like mobile phones or tablet computers, have rechargeable batteries inside.

This girl is charging her mobile phone from an electrical outlet.

THINGS THAT USE BATTERIES

Look around your home and school. What can you find that uses batteries?

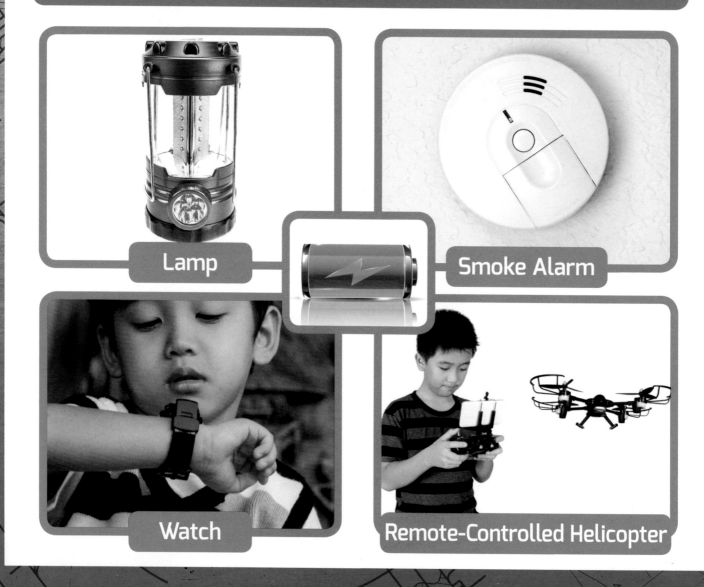

Lamp

Smoke Alarm

Watch

Remote-Controlled Helicopter

A battery-powered flashlight helps us to see in the dark.

Flashlights use batteries to power a bulb inside the flashlight and shine light out.

LIGHT BULBS

Candles are helpful when the power goes out!

Before light bulbs were **invented**, people used candles to light their homes. Now, people use electricity to light their homes.

Light bulbs do more than help us see in the dark. They can also tell us important things.

These traffic lights tell us when it is safe to cross the road.

HOW LIGHT BULBS WORK

All light bulbs need a source of power to work. This might be from a battery or from the grid power supply.

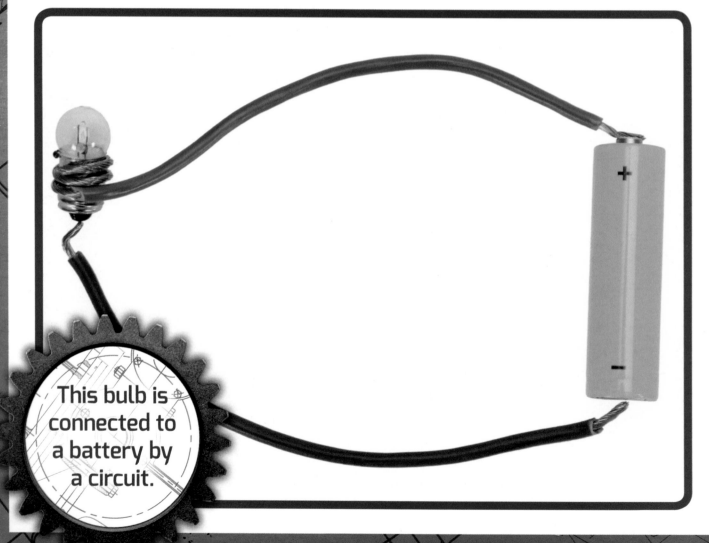

This bulb is connected to a battery by a circuit.

Light bulbs can get very hot when they are on.

Light bulbs need electricity to work. Inside a light bulb, the electrical energy is changed into light and heat.

Filament

The **filament** is what makes the light bulb shine.

When electricity passes through the filament, it gets hot and glows. This makes the light bulb shine.

The outside of a light bulb is made of clear glass or plastic. This lets the light shine out. The outside of a bulb can sometimes be colored, changing the color of the light.

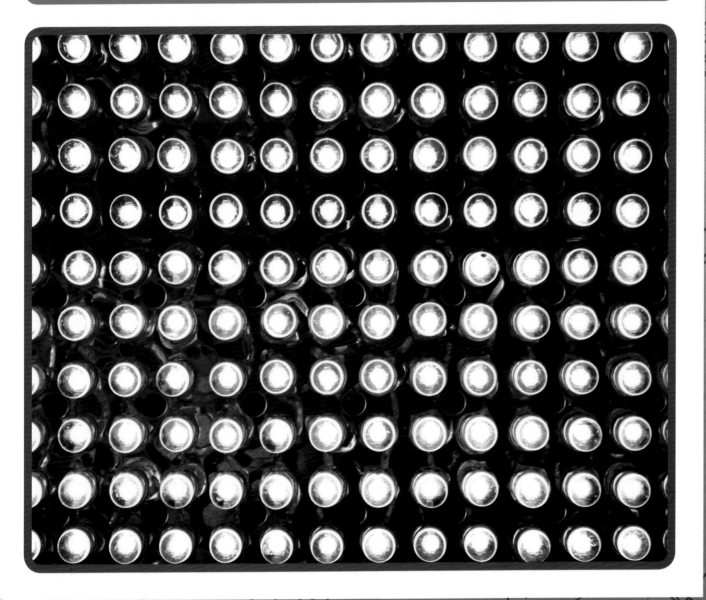

DIFFERENT TYPES OF LIGHT BULBS

Bulbs can come in different shapes and sizes. They all have different uses.

Different Light Bulbs

Energy-Saving Bulb

Halogen bulbs give off a very bright light. Compact fluorescent bulbs use less energy and last longer than other types of bulbs.

THINGS THAT USE LIGHT BULBS

This miner uses a headlamp to see underground.

Your TV might have a light on it to tell you if it is on or off. This uses a small bulb.

Some bulbs are used to display things like the time.
Digital displays use tiny bulbs called LEDs.

GLOSSARY

circuit	a path for electric current to travel around
container	something to put things in
energy	the power from electricity to make things work
filament	a small piece of wire in a light bulb
grid power	the general-purpose power supply that is often supplied directly to homes
invented	made something new
portable	able to be moved or carried
terminals	the parts of a battery that join it to a circuit

INDEX